THINK LIKE A FUTURIST

HOW TO PLAN AROUND UNCERTAINTY AND FUTURE-PROOF YOUR BUSINESS

SCOTT STEINBERG
WWW.AKEYNOTESPEAKER.COM

BROUGHT TO YOU BY:

WWW.AKEYNOTESPEAKER.COM

WWW.BIZDEVASSOCIATION.COM

WWW.AKEYNOTESPEAKER.COM/FUTURETRENDS

ACCELERATE. INNOVATE. TRANSFORM.

FAST FORWARD

How to Turbo-Charge *Business*, *Sales*, and *Career Growth*™

SCOTT STEINBERG
BESTSELLING AUTHOR OF MAKE CHANGE WORK FOR YOU™

Put Yourself on the
Fast-Track to Success

Q4 2020

www.AKeynoteSpeaker.com

PUBLISHED BY:
BLUEPRINT: YOUR NEW ROADMAP TO SUCCESS™

THINK LIKE A FUTURIST™

1ST EDITION
© 2020 HOW MEDIA LLC

ALL RIGHTS RESERVED. NO PART OF THIS PUBLICATION MAY BE REPRODUCED, DISTRIBUTED, STORED, OR TRANSMITTED IN ANY FORM OR BY ANY MEANS (INCLUDING BUT NOT LIMITED TO) ELECTRONIC, MECHANICAL, PHOTOCOPYING, RECORDING, OR OTHERWISE WITHOUT THE PRIOR WRITTEN PERMISSION OF BOTH THE COPYRIGHT OWNER AND THE ABOVE PUBLISHER OF THE BOOK.

ALL PRODUCT NAMES, TRADEMARKS, AND REGISTERED TRADEMARKS ARE PROPERTY OF THEIR RESPECTIVE OWNERS. ALL COMPANY, PRODUCT, AND SERVICE NAMES USED ARE FOR IDENTIFICATION PURPOSES ONLY. USE OF THESE NAMES, TRADEMARKS, AND BRANDS DOES NOT IMPLY ENDORSEMENT.

DEDICATION
T, Z, N AND CO., WHO CONSTANTLY INSPIRE US TO POSITIVE CHANGE AND DISRUPTION.

TIME AND THE WORLD DO NOT STAND STILL. **CHANGE IS THE LAW OF LIFE. AND THOSE WHO LOOK ONLY TO THE PAST OR PRESENT ARE CERTAIN TO MISS THE FUTURE.**

- JOHN F. KENNEDY

INTRO

As noted in *Make Change Work for You*, our bestselling guide to trendspotting and innovation, unpredictability is the only thing we can predict and uncertainty the only certain for working professionals going forward. From the smallest local businesses to the largest global enterprises, the mass onset of coronavirus and other disruptive events will only continue to impact the fundamental way in which countless individuals and organizations do business in coming years. From the methods we use to manage development and distribution, to the way we market and sell products, make no mistake. Massive shifts in operating models, technology, and professional best practices promise to permanently redefine the way we all do business, and connect and communicate in the workplace, for decades to come.

Working as futurists and trends experts for today's largest household brands and organizations, our firm FutureProof Strategies has partnered with hundreds of Fortune 500 leaders and associations to help identify rising trends and build business strategies designed to capitalize on emerging opportunities. But after spending over 20 years focused on answering one pivotal question – *What's coming next?* – we've also discovered that learning to future-proof a business or brand is also far less difficult and time-consuming than most would suspect. Inside the following guide, you'll find a number of forward-thinking strategies and solutions for helping yourself and your organization stay ahead of the curve, and teaching yourself how to spot and capitalize on opportunities before rivals can react. It's our hope that it proves an essential tool in your efforts to plan around uncertainty, future-proof your business, and build a career roadmap that can withstand any unexpected twist or turn that the market takes.

While we can't always say for certain what the future will bring, it bears reminding. We always have the ability to think ahead, plan in advance, and – even if we should find ourselves unprepared for whatever happens – steer the future towards more positive outcomes by actively exercising a little ingenuity and hard work. Furthermore, even when surprise happenings and events call the best-laid plans into question, don't forget: You can always learn from every circumstance and pivot accordingly. True: We live in extraordinary and eventful times. But as you'll see time and again throughout this guide, you don't have to be psychic to see what's coming around the corner. More importantly, a little flexibility (and strategy) is all it often takes to successfully bridge the gap from where you're looking to go to where you're at.

— Scott Steinberg

For more on how to future-proof yourself and fast-track success, also be sure to check out our new book *FAST >> FORWARD: How to Turbo-Charge Business, Sales, and Career Growth*™.

HOW TO THINK LIKE A FUTURIST

You say you want to get better at planning around uncertainty, future-proofing your business and career, and learning to stay one step ahead of the curve?

No surprise there: While we'd all like to improve our ability to see what's coming next, it often seems difficult to anticipate what's coming around the bend. But despite common misperceptions, the good news is that in actuality, it's far easier and far less time-consuming than most of us would suspect. Better yet, you don't even have to be particularly talented or brilliant to do so either. So allow me to share a trade secret: You don't actually need to be a futurist in order to think like one. More than anything else, the key is simply *knowing where to look for answers, the right questions to ask*, and *whom to turn to for insight*.

Just ask Germany's Association for Chemistry and Economics (the VCW), which has over 30,000 members spread across hundreds of industries worldwide. Knowing that teamwork would be crucial to successfully staying one step ahead of the curve, and accelerating the speed at which it could adapt, the VCW recently wanted to create a solution that would allow these members to get better about working together to anticipate the future – and drive innovation on a huge scale. In addition, it was looking for a tool that would allow these folks to more easily with collaborate scientists in other fields as well.

Amusingly though, as intimidating as the prospect sounds, after studying the shape of the challenge before it, the VCW realized that all it had to do to get better about spotting new opportunities – and send its prospects soaring – was just bring a little ingenuity to bear. Because in the end, what the association wound up doing was simply coining the concept of "Social Chemistry," and building an open online portal that allowed members to crowdsource ideas, team up with talent from outside the field, and pool resources across public and private organizations as needed. Incredibly, within just 5 weeks, not only was the VCW able to identify numerous trends and investment opportunities which weren't even remotely on the association's radar. It was also able to pinpoint hundreds of promising new ideas to explore, and spark dozens of new initiatives for the industry – not bad for a small, cost-affordable website.

As you can see, when it comes to maximizing your insight – and maximizing your opportunities – you don't necessarily have to be a genius to get ahead in business anymore... rather, just a little bit more clever and *ingenious* instead. Likewise, finding success today is less about being the most accomplished person in the room and more about being the one who's mastered the art of learning how to most quickly and effectively learn about any given topic instead as well. Moreover, when it comes to finding winning ideas to pursue, you don't have to be exceptionally talented or creative either. Rather, just the type of leader who prizes diversity of thought and opinion, and actively makes a point to surround themselves with an army of trusted advisers by making leadership a concept that scales.

In effect, as much as we all love celebrating the Elon Musks and Steve Jobs of the world, succeeding in a business environment that's as fast-changing and unpredictable as today's marketplace isn't about having to be a single-minded or visionary leader anymore. Instead, it's about being able to draw upon the wisdom of crowds more frequently, and becoming more of what experts call an *anticipatory leader*[1] ... Someone who's not only more skilled at anticipating the future, but also more clever and resilient when it comes to helping an organization consistently steer itself toward success no matter what the future brings.

But let's not get ahead of ourselves just yet. If you don't mind, before proceeding, I'd like to back up a little bit and start our examination of the ancient art of trendspotting by asking a simple question: *What is a Futurist?* I won't be offended if you roll your eyes here. After all, a lot of folks tend to think of us as the corporate version of late-night psychics. But the idea that we're in the business of reading tarot cards and tea leaves couldn't be further from the truth.

In fact – and I probably shouldn't tell you this – our dirty secret is that futurists don't actually predict the future for a living. Rather, we carefully study the current state of the market and society, as well as patterns and trends that appear to be slowly percolating

---

1. *The Anticipatory Leader: Futurist, Strategist, and Integrator* – Anika Savage and Michael Sales

upwards across both – then consider how likely it is that various developments will take shape, and the degree to which they'll impact any given organization. By doing so, we're able to challenge partners to think more critically about various scenarios – and how to create an action plan designed to deal with any given development that might come to pass.

Truth be told, we're market researchers and anthropologists more than anything else. Ultimately, we spend most of our time collecting data, analyzing information, and crafting scenarios that organizations can simulate working through to prepare themselves to greet new challenges. Put simply, it's our job to get business leaders to carefully consider which way that the future is trending – and help them determine which strategic direction to go in, as well as the best plan of attack to adopt. And you'd be amazed at the kind of insights you can surface when you apply similar approaches in thinking.

For example, a few years back, Coca-Cola Australia put on its futurist thinking cap and decided to study the shape of changing consumer markets, and quickly noticed that Millennials and Gen Zers were rapidly becoming two of the largest audiences for its carbonated beverages. In addition, they also realized that these younger audiences – having been raised on the Internet and social networks – were less likely to engage in face-to-face interaction than previous generations. So over time, when young adults in Australia inevitably started getting together more often online than in real-life, and stopped drinking its soft drink products as much as in the past, the company was already well aware that it needed to radically reinvent its strategy to connect with them both online and off.

But rather than take out millions in TV or radio advertising, which it had already researched and realized wouldn't connect with digital natives? And rather than try and cook up all sorts of crazy new flavors, which it knew wouldn't fix the bigger underlying problem it faced? Coca-Cola instead decided to bridge the gap between the digital and physical worlds by printing the 150 most popular Australian boys' and girls' first names on Coke bottles (bottles it was already manufacturing and selling) and —via cost-effective social, online, and mobile media programs— invited citizens to share them and strike up a conversation, online and off.

Incredibly, within 3 months, the business had successfully blanked the entire country and increased consumption among young adults by double digits. As you may have noticed, the campaign proved to be so clever and cost-effective that it later came to the U.S. and other territories in a big way as well. As you can see, a little advance planning and forethought can be a powerful tool for helping drive ongoing growth and success for any given business.

On the bright side though, like I was saying earlier, if you're hoping to become more of what management consultants Anika Savage and Michael Sales call an anticipatory leader, it may help to know that you don't need specialized training to do a futurist's job, though – or even a good publicist. In fact, as one of my peers put it, the truth is that we are all futurists at heart. After all, when we get married, it's not uncommon to assume that it will last a lifetime, and when we make an investment, it's not uncommon to think it will pay off in the long run, as futurist Sheryl Connelly reminds. But as we're all aware, these assumptions often don't pan out the way we anticipate. Which is exactly why we often find ourselves asking: What would we do if things changed and didn't go according to plan… how would we rethink our operating strategies as well? In effect, that's precisely what a futurist does – so congratulations, I'm officially giving you all a promotion. In case you're not busy doing enough different things at work these days, you can add yet another skill to your resume.

Anyways, as a working professional, you're no doubt already asking yourself all sorts of questions about what's coming next for various industries every day. So if you want to think like a futurist more effectively going forward? Mostly, all you need to do is make a point to ask more pointed questions here – and make a game of asking *WHAT IF?* at every turn, planning for an even wider range of eventualities. After all, the deeper the research you do, and more you practice mapping out specific actions that you can take in case unforeseen events suddenly upend your business plan, the more successful you'll be. And, of course, the more that you make a habit of regularly simulating and role-playing through scenarios such as these? The more you'll discover that the type of critical thinking futurists use is simply a basic mental muscle of sorts – and, like any muscle, is one that you can both get in the reflexive habit of using, and strengthen through repeat exercise.

For instance, we recently completed a project for the PGA that took a closer look at the future of golf. Unfortunately, as successful as this 600 year-old sport has been, it's having trouble connecting with young people, who see it as too time-consuming, too expensive, too elitist, too outdated, and too tough to master. But younger generations will become the largest audience for the game within 5 years, though – and would anyone care to guess what their average attention span is? It's 8 seconds. A goldfish's is 9 seconds by comparison. (Thanks *Fortnite* and Snapchat!)

So given that some of you probably have teens and twenty-somethings at home, some pointed questions you might ask yourself are: How likely are these young bucks to spend 4 minutes engaged in any given activity, let alone 4 hours lounging around a fairway? How many are open to blowing $50 on a round of golf, not counting clothes, lessons, and equipment? And how many would prefer just casually hanging out and chatting with their friends in an online game to waking up early and teeing off at some stuffy country club anyway?

It doesn't take a rocket scientist to see that fundamental sea changes are happening here that innovations like better equipment and cooler shoes alone won't solve. Or that the sport doesn't exactly lend itself towards the short-form and social experiences that today's youths thrive on. Which is precisely why businesses like TopGolf and Drive Shack asked themselves another, equally important question: *What if we just made playing the sport of golf simpler – and helped people get to the fun parts of the game sooner? And, in doing so, quickly became the hottest thing happening in the industry today.*

If you haven't visited, you can think of these one-stop entertainment destinations – which combine high-tech driving ranges with restaurants, sports bars, and event spaces – as being equivalent to the sport of golf as what Dave & Busters is to traditional video game arcades. But as much as these firms have capitalized on cutting-edge technologies to grow their business, never mind smart viewscreens and micro-chipped balls... I'd argue that their core innovation is simply introducing a business model that makes the golfing experience shorter, more social, and more accessible to everyone. Again, a little bit of critical thinking is all it often takes to see the future taking shape more clearly, and a knack for asking better questions is all it takes to successfully plan around it.

However, if you want to become more of an anticipatory leader (someone who's capable of coming up with game changing solutions like these in coming years) it's also important to note. The trick to getting ahead going forward isn't just being able to accurately envision future scenarios, then think backwards and create a working roadmaps that bridge the gap from here to there. It's to also accept that other, alternate forces are in play and futures are constantly taking shape – and design your business and operating strategies in such a way that you've got multiple backup plans that you can put in motion if you suddenly need to rip up your playbook and rewrite it on the fly. Flexibility is the essence of future-proofing, as I always say.

So if you want to get better about planning for tomorrow, it's not enough to just get good at assessing various business and investment opportunities anymore. You've also got to make a point to get good at *exercising strong, but weakly held opinions* going forward. In other words, we're all going to be asked to make more important decisions on the fly going forward – even as, in such fast-changing times, the business intelligence we have to call upon becomes increasingly less reliable. So in addition to doing your homework as extensively as possible, and using the best information available when it comes to picking new business opportunities or new ventures to add to your portfolio? It's also vital that you keep enough of an open mind and eye on what's coming next that you're able to consistently revise these decisions as new information is gained. Considering that nine out of 10 companies – especially start-ups – who make it in the market tend to succeed with different business plans than those they first envisioned? Again, it pays to recognize that part of being a successful business leader in coming years won't just be about picking the right horses to back. It also means knowing when it's time to stop digging in your heels and start thinking about how to turn on a dime instead.

Consider the case of Korean auto manufacturer Hyundai. A decade ago, its low-cost, high-quality vehicles were just starting to grow in popularity in US, and its fortunes were on the rise. But when the Great Recession hit, and it was suddenly and unexpectedly pummeled by a drop in consumer spending? Out of nowhere, it found that it had to quickly pump its brakes and veer in a different direction.

Unlike competitors though, Hyundai didn't immediately bump up ad spending or promote new product features or incentives. Instead, the company decided to be more strategic about looking for new opportunities, and created a program that allowed its salespeople and showroom employees (everyday frontline workers) to speak up and share their insights more readily. Hyundai then asked these workers to poll customers to find out what was going on, and discovered that the reason for spending drops had nothing to do with product feature sets or perceptions of overall quality – rather it was the risk that customers saw associated with buying big-ticket items like automobiles in such uncertain times.

So instead of giving a knee-jerk response, and slashing price tags, Hyundai decided to slash risks for its customers instead, and started promoting a no-strings-attached money-back refund if shoppers lost their job for any reason within the next 12 months. As a result, the company's sales doubled in January 2009, while the industry's plummeted nearly 50%, biggest drop since 1963 – not too shabby for a slight shift in steering, right? What's more, in case you hadn't noticed, everything old is apparently new again: In the midst of coronavirus-related concerns, a number of auto manufacturers are currently running similar promotions as we speak.

Of course, as any business leader can tell you, it's difficult trying to anticipate the future in a world that changes as often as the one we live in today, and these types of predictions will only get tougher to make going forward.

But while the practice of engaging in futurism – making a point to actively contemplate future events and trends, and how they promise to impact you and your ventures – is becoming increasingly challenging? Futurism is also an important talent to get comfortable exercising, because it's a growingly critical skill for any working professional to master, especially when far-ranging decisions need making.

As a reminder, not only will the next 10 years bring more change than the prior 10,000 – change we'll all have to plan around. More than half of Fortune 500 firms will also be replaced by the time that 2030 arrives. In addition, thanks to our friends in the startup community, it now takes most organizations less than 30 days to deploy new products and business ideas, causing the lifespan of even today's most accomplished firms to shrink to just a single decade.

So if you want to enjoy any longevity as a business leader in coming years? It means that talent and smarts alone won't be enough to thrive in a world where even winners aren't surefire long-term bets anymore. Instead, like anticipatory leaders are aware, you'll also have to be far more proactive and agile when it comes to addressing emerging developments in the market. And more and more, the ability to successfully anticipate what's coming around the bend, and how to deal with what's coming next, will mean the difference between disrupting or being disrupted.

Anyhow, if you want to become more of an anticipatory leader, it's no surprise that you'll have to start thinking like a futurist more often. And that not only means having to teach yourself to get better at weighing every decision. It also means having to craft more adaptable business plans as you go. Happily, asking yourself three simple questions can help as you go about considering how to build a more future-proof strategy, including:

- Financial gains aside, how can you always ensure you're finding ways to win from every opportunity – i.e. by gaining new capabilities, insights, and resources that can be applied to other business ventures?

- What level of flexibility do potential ventures you choose to undertake allow – and just how readily can you repurpose tools, technologies, and insights from them in new and novel ways if needed... or use them to quickly pivot or springboard to new opportunities?

- How successfully and rapidly can resources and learnings garnered from your efforts in any given area translate to other contexts, industries, or areas of business opportunity?

In effect, what I'm asking you to is look beyond balance sheets and research reports alone and always consider – how well does this investment bolster and augment my overall business strategy and/or holdings? And if sudden, unexpected developments call even the best-laid plans into question, how much room to maneuver do different opportunities truly afford me? As you may have noticed, no matter how much time and money you can afford to invest in any given venture, more often, if there's one thing you can always bank on, it's the benefits to be recognized by exercising start-up-level ingenuity at every turn.

On the bright side, as we've discussed, you can certainly get better about anticipating the future by exercising a more forward-thinking mindset. Noting this, more than anything, three skills you'll want to cultivate more frequently going forward are *critical analysis, inquisitiveness,* and *imagination* – the ability to consistently ask *Why, How,* and *What If* at every turn, as it were. Doing so won't just help you practice the art of futurism more readily. It will also help give you the perspective you need to determine where holes in the marketplace (and holes in your investment portfolio) exist, plus the insight needed to make smarter decisions going forward.

Likewise, as we briefly touched on before, you can also improve your odds of finding success by embracing the wisdom of the crowd wherever possible. That's because change is now happening on a global and epic scale – and the more radically you can multiply the resources that are available to you, the more radically you can multiply the speed at which you can solve any given challenge. In essence, the key is getting ahead going forward isn't just to get good at evaluating business plans and financial models, but also to get good at researching, networking, and applying insights in context.

Because to stay on top of emerging trends, you've not only got to stay up to speed on what's happening in different markets. At the rate and scale that change can impact us today, you've also got to build a community of expert advisors around you who can help you stay better attuned to impending shifts, get smarter about any given topic faster, and operate at much greater scope if you want to stay competitive. After all, you might not know much about quantum computing or advanced robotics... But when it comes to staying on top of new developments in these spaces and evaluating new investment opportunities, which can pop up anytime, anywhere all over the world? It pays to have a really smart group of friends you can call upon who do.

Ultimately though, if you're looking for some quick, simple things that you can do from a personal standpoint to sharpen your future senses, there are five simple activities you can engage in if you want to get better at spotting and interpreting signals that the market is sending[2], according to leading futurists:.

> • **STAY UP-TO-DATE ON TRENDS** – A number of high-level socioeconomic and technological forces called megatrends promise to impact the future at all times – and you should be monitoring them at every turn, say industry experts. For example: Millennials – who think, learn, and operate differently from prior generations – are becoming the largest demographic in the workforce, just as artificial intelligence and robotics are transforming the shape of the workplace as we speak. Just a few ways you can stay on top of megatrends include reading up on the latest news, attending conferences, staying attuned to academic research, speaking with end-users and

2. *https://hpmegatrends.com/5-tips-to-think-like-a-futurist-f5ebae3e404d?gi=3606e26583d7*

industry thought leaders, maintaining contacts across industry supply chains, and keeping on top of startup and investment activity. No matter how high a level that you find yourself operating at, never forget that grassroots research can yield tremendous insights, and you should never be too busy to engage in it.

• **IMAGINE TOMORROW TAKING SHAPE** – Once you've spotted an emerging trend, make a point to think ahead and imagine what the future looks like 3, 5, and 10 years hence for an industry or market. Now work backwards and consider how it arrived there. Ask yourself questions about which trends prompted these shifts and their timing, as well as market conditions, business models, and technologies that came into play during these transitions. Now think about how you and your company can play a role in helping the market arrive at this future state. In the case of self-driving cars, for example, you might ask: How will current markets and industries be impacted by these vehicles? What business models will they upend – and to what extent? And what new opportunities will their arrival create?

• **TAKE A STRUCTURED APPROACH TO ANALYSIS** – Having a strategic methodology for evaluating opportunities is essential. For example: You might start by deciding whether a new technology is an incremental innovation (such as a new feature or function) or disruptive innovation that produces a new product, service, or category. Afterwards, you could then identify prospective markets and audiences for it; pick a time period to examine; and put the idea through rigorous analysis to understand the business opportunity it introduces. Then you'll also want to consider the potential value to your organization, and the strategic rationale for pursuing it. In other words, it's all about right-sizing opportunities here – and once you've right-sized a concept, you can work backwards to put a tactical plan of action steps in place that can help you start achieving it if you decide it's something that you wish to pursue.

• **EMBRACE INVERSE APPROACHES TO INNOVATION** – Great ideas can come from anywhere, right? That's why more organizations are practicing both outside-in and inside-out innovation. For example, many are turning to the concept of open innovation – inviting feedback and ideas from external sources such as the startup and academic communities (i.e. the outside in) – as a means of scaling and accelerating innovation. Likewise, others are turning to inside-out methods and taking tools and technologies that they've come up – i.e. platforms for data sharing and collaboration that they've developed – and incorporating them into others' innovation processes. Learning to effectively leverage both will become increasingly important in coming years.

• **MOVE FROM ANALYTICS TO ACTION** – With over 20 billion devices now talking to each other, data is the lifeblood of any modern organization. But studies tell us that less than 10% of relevant information is currently being used to enhance organizational value. Bearing this in mind, it's vital to become more data literate too, and tap into the mountain of information that's increasingly being collected by many of our businesses. After all, artificially-intelligent software programs can help you spot emerging patterns and leading indicators faster than the human eye. So as you go about envisioning the future? Don't forget to get technical as well. Not only should you have standardized data management systems in place that can help you aggregate and analyze information at every turn. You should also be leveraging AI-powered assistants to help you quickly go from analytics to actionable advice at a glance.

On the bright side, as you can see, while it pays to apply both qualitative and quantitative measures to weighing investments, learning to operate like a futurist doesn't require specialized skills or training. In fact, it's more about exercising critical thinking and creativity—the type of talents most of you have been honing your entire career. Lean into these types of forward-looking skills further, and you too can discover what it takes to see ahead of the curve.

However, that said, if you want to translate these insights into business gains, do be advised as well. It's also important to note that becoming an anticipatory leader requires more than just exercising your imagination and possessing a good instinct for where things are headed tomorrow. Rather, as authors Savage and Sales note, it demands thinking in three dimensions: As a Futurist, Strategist, and Integrator.

FUTURISTS, as we discussed, act as curators of sorts, (a) exploring developments in various industries, sciences, and markets (b) collecting ideas from conventional and obscure sources and (c) tracking patterns and trends to understand how they impact an organization.

STRATEGISTS see the possibilities that each trend holds, and can weave disparate information sources into useful connections and combinations. They build high-level strategies that tie these insights together to create positive business results.

INTEGRATORS go beyond observing and analyzing, and translate understanding into action – in other words, they know how to work within organizational systems, and inspire colleagues to produce positive results.

As you might note, to be an anticipatory leader means not only being able to see systems –industries, markets, etc. – as networks of interacting forces, and understanding the cause-and-effect relationships that these forces create. It also means being able to determine where these dynamics present opportunities for growth and innovation – and being able to take complex concepts and break them down into tactical day-to-day steps that an organization can take to achieve its goals.

Of course, when it comes to crafting real-world solutions, adapting your future insights into actionable strategies can be every bit as challenging as trying to spot the next big thing in business. So from a strategic perspective, it also pays to keep in mind a few handy tips and principles that can help you go from insight to innovation.

- **USING TIME CONES, NOT TIMELINES –**
Many experts recommend using time cones, not timelines, when doing future projections, such as quantitative futurist Amy Webb[3]. According to Webb, organizations often like to use fixed strategic timelines based around round numbers – e.g. 5- or 10-year plans – when doing high-level planning, because they're easy to communicate and categorize. But rather than used fixed timelines, as they're highly inflexible, and unexpected changes and disruptive events can often fall outside of their scope, she says, it's often better to use time cones when doing strategy planning instead. The process starts by sketching out your thoughts on four different categories: (1) Tactics (2) Strategy (3) Vision and (4) Systems-Level Evolution.

    o Tactics help us plan specific actions for the next 12-24 months, since we have a good idea of what the next year or two will bring.
    o Strategy asks us to examine the general direction the organization will take over the next 2-5 years in terms of defining priorities and allocating resources.

    o Vision's 5-10 year scope refers to areas in which we choose to pursue research, make long-term investments, and develop tomorrow's workforce.

    o And Systems-Level Evolution planning asks us to take a closer look at how industries must evolve to meet rising technology and regulatory challenges, as well as challenges related to megatrends and similar forces.

3. https://hbr.org/2019/07/how-to-do-strategic-planning-like-a-futurist

A more flexible way to represent the future as it unfolds, notes Webb, time cones also offer greater room for your plans to change and evolve as more information is gained.

• **APPLYING FOUR STRATEGIC PRINCIPLES –** In addition, if you want to train yourself to get in the mindset of a futurist more readily, you can do so by applying several basic strategic principles, says Marina Gorbis, executive director for the Institute for the Future:

1. FOCUS ON TRENDS, NOT FADS – As discussed earlier, anticipating the future is a process of looking at complex, interrelated events and the connections between them – not simply studying the temporary effects that they're producing. So be sure you're staying laser-focused on the big picture at all times. A handy way to picture this concept, according to Gorbis, is to think about the difference between waves and tides. Waves are fleeting events that come and go – what we see on the surface, she says. But an anticipatory leader trains themselves to see tides – the deeper forces or megatrends at work happening underneath the surface that are causing these waves, or disturbances, in the market. For example: The fact that Taylor Swift's songs can still hit #1 on the charts, but not sell a million copies anymore is concerning. However, the changes in consumers' basic digital media habits and growth in online streaming services that are causing these sales to fall? Now that's a more important point to stay tuned into. Your goal, says Gorbis, is to determine which forces are at work at all times, how they impact the marketplace, and where you have the opportunity to shape the future for the positive.

2. KEEP A LOOKOUT FOR SIGNALS – The future is constantly changing. Unfortunately, historical data (which is mostly what we have) is notoriously unreliable at predicting it when things are in a state of change – especially if we're at radical inflection points, notes Gorbis. That's why paying attention to signals, which are little developments happening on the margins (things that may even look weird or strange to you) is important, she says. In effect, a signal is "a small or local innovation or disruption such as a new product, market strategy, or technology that has the potential to grow in scale and geographic distribution." For example: The rise of biometrics – body- and face-tracking technology – hasn't completely upended the market yet, but it's rapidly being deployed at airports, laboratories, and manufacturing centers worldwide, and will cause a seismic impact in coming years. Futurists get in the habit of looking for signals like this constantly.

3. WATCH FOR EMERGING PATTERNS – The point of aggregating signals and determining how they connect to bigger-picture trends is to help us spot emerging patterns, reminds Gorbis. These patterns help tell a larger story – and point to where the future will head. By observing them, you can see which tools, technologies, and business models are on the decline, and which are on the rise. For example, looking at the media sector, we can see we're moving from an age where big institutions such as corporations and news conglomerates control the flow of information to one where platforms such as Twitter – wherein large numbers of individuals operating independently are openly crowdsourcing journalism – are democratizing it instead.

4. CREATE EXPERT COMMUNITIES –
No one alone can accurately predict the future 100% of the time. Rather, as we discussed earlier, if you want to improve your accuracy, these days it's more of a collaborative and communal affair. This requires us to cultivate diversity of thought and perspective amongst our teams, and involve experts from many different domains when making decisions. And the more you can create a network of diverse people boasting different backgrounds and experiences who can help provide more robust feedback and insight when you're working to envision the future, says Gorbis? The more successful that you'll be. For instance, if you visit websites like Challenge.gov, you'll see that even agencies like the EPA and NASA – which are staffed by some of the world's brightest minds – are putting up cash bounties and contests asking the general public for help developing tomorrow's most advanced technology solutions.

Ultimately, what we find is that practicing the art of futurism isn't about having to predict the future. Rather, it's about thinking more deeply about complex issues, connecting signals into larger patterns, using these patterns to imagine new possibilities, and aligning groups of people towards achieving the common goal of putting all these promising new ideas in motion.

And while the concept of becoming an anticipatory leader may be relatively new, keep in mind. The futurist thinking skills it champions will only become more important to exercise in the face of growing industry change and disruption going forward. Happily, the more you practice applying the art of futurism, and more frequently you strive to make leadership a concept that scales? The more skilled at spotting seemingly disparate connections that you'll become, and more successful you'll ultimately be.

In short, like we touched on before, you don't have to be smarter, more talented, or more of a creative genius to spot the future taking shape. Instead, you simply need to know where to look for answers, the right questions to ask, and whom to turn to for insight if you want to get better about seeing around the corner. And the more you make a point to exercise all the skills and talents we've discussed here? The more you'll be able to improve your odds of spotting what's coming next, and the better equipped you'll also be to stay ahead of the curve as well – no matter what the future may bring.

FUTURE PLANNING WORKSHOP: STRATEGY IN MOTION

REQUIRED TIME: 60-90 MINUTES

INSTRUCTIONS:

1. CREATE A TWO-SENTENCE SUMMARY AND MISSION STATEMENT FOR A SAMPLE BUSINESS

2. BRAINSTORM 10 UNEXPECTED NEW DEVELOPMENTS (UNFORESEEN EVENTS OR HAPPENINGS) THAT MIGHT IMPACT THIS BUSINESS IN THE FUTURE – THEN PLACE EACH UNEXPECTED DEVELOPMENT ON A NOTECARD, ONE PER NOTECARD

3. DIVIDE EXERCISE PARTICIPANTS INTO TABLES OF 5-8 INDIVIDUALS FROM DIFFERENT ORGANIZATIONS, DEPARTMENTS, AND LEVELS OF SENIORITY

4. GIVE EACH TABLE A FLIPCHART TO TAKE NOTES ON, AND ASK EACH TABLE TO ASSIGN A LEADER WHO WILL TAKE NOTES AND PRESENT ANY FINDINGS

5. PRESENT THE AUDIENCE WITH AN OVERVIEW OF THE SAMPLE BUSINESS YOU'VE BUILT, THEN GIVE EACH TABLE 5 MINUTES TO COME UP WITH A BUSINESS PLAN AND INVESTMENT STRATEGY FOR THIS FAUX ORGANIZATION

6. EVERY 5 MINUTES, ASK ONE MEMBER OF EACH TABLE TO COME UP AND PICK A NOTECARD CONTAINING AN UNEXPECTED DEVELOPMENT AND READ IT ALOUD TO THE ENTIRE GROUP

7. ONCE THEY'VE PICKED AN UNEXPECTED DEVELOPMENT, ASK EACH TABLE TO TAKE 5 MINUTES TO WRITE UP THEIR THOUGHTS ON HOW IT IMPACTS THEIR BUSINESS PLAN ON THE FLIPCHARTS – AND HOW THEY CAN ADAPT TO IT

8. AFTER REPEATING THIS PROCESS 8-10 TIMES, ASK ALL TABLES TO TAKE 5 MINUTES TO SUMMARIZE THEIR FINDINGS ON A SINGLE FLIPCHART PAGE

9. THEN, ONE-BY-ONE, ASK EACH TABLE LEADER TO TAKE 2-3 MINUTES TO STAND UP AND PRESENT THEIR FINDINGS TO THE ENTIRE ROOM

10. QUICKLY SUMMARIZE THE GROUP'S FINDINGS FOR YOUR AUDIENCE, AND COLLECT FLIPCHARTS (WHICH SHOULD BE FULL OF IDEAS AND INSIGHTS) FOR LATER USE

SAMPLE BUSINESS

PULSE CAPITAL

- OPERATES $500 FUTURECARE CAPITAL INVESTMENT FUND

- PULSE CAPITAL INVESTS IN EARLY GROWTH, REVENUE-STAGE FIRMS THAT ARE LEVERAGING EMERGING TECHNOLOGIES TO RETHINK THE FUTURE OF WELLNESS AND HEALTHCARE.

UNEXPECTED DEVELOPMENTS

FEVERISH THINKING

A GLOBAL PANDEMIC CAUSES WIDESPREAD DISRUPTION TO YOUR SUPPLY CHAIN

SEEING GREEN
ECO-CONSCIOUSNESS AND GREEN SOLUTIONS COME TO THE FOREFRONT OF CONSUMER SENTIMENT

GOING FOR BROKE

WORLDWIDE ECONOMIES BEGIN TO LAPSE INTO RECESSION, AND INVESTOR CONFIDENCE QUICKLY PULLS BACK

SOMEBODY'S WATCHING ME
PRIVACY AND IDENTITY CONCERNS OVERWHEMINGLY TREND AND DOMINATE MEDIA HEADLINES

THIS MEANS WAR
ROGUE NATIONS' UNPREDICTABLE ACTIONS CAUSE ENTIRE REGIONS OF THE WORLD TO BE THROWN INTO CHAOS

ROCKING THE VOTE
POLITICAL UPHEAVAL ROCKS THE MARKETPLACE, AND LEADS TO MOUNTING UNCERTAINTY

BENDING THE RULES
NEW REGULATIONS TAKE EFFECT THAT GREATLY INHIBIT YOUR ABILITY TO DO BUSINESS

CASHING OUT

UNMOVED BY YOUR CURRENT PERFORMANCE, INVESTORS SUDDENLY BEGIN MAKING DIFFERENT SUCCESS METRICS A PRIORITY

ADDITIONAL NOTES

DISCUSSION GUIDE: ACCELERATING GROWTH + INNOVATION

REQUIRED TIME: 60-90 MINUTES

INSTRUCTIONS:

1. CREATE A ONE-SENTENCE WRITE-UP OF 10 MEGATRENDS THAT PROMISE TO RESHAPE A CHOSEN INDUSTRY – THEN PLACE EACH MEGATREND ON A NOTECARD, ONE PER NOTECARD

2. BRAINSTORM 10 QUESTIONS THAT YOU'D ALSO LIKE TO ASK PARTICIPANTS ABOUT HOW EACH OF THESE MEGATRENDS MIGHT EVOLVE AND IMPACT THEIR BUSINESS – THEN PLACE EACH QUESTION ON A PRESENTATION SLIDE, ONE PER SLIDE

3. DIVIDE EXERCISE PARTICIPANTS INTO TABLES OF 5-8 INDIVIDUALS FROM DIFFERENT ORGANIZATIONS, DEPARTMENTS, AND LEVELS OF SENIORITY

4. GIVE EACH TABLE A FLIPCHART TO TAKE NOTES ON, AND ASK EACH TABLE TO ASSIGN A LEADER WHO WILL TAKE NOTES AND PRESENT ANY FINDINGS

5. ASK THE LEADER FROM EACH TABLE TO COME UP AND PICK A SINGLE NOTECARD CONTAINING A MEGATREND, WHICH THEIR TABLE WILL BE ASSIGNED TO COVER

6. EVERY 5 MINUTES, ASK A QUESTION FROM ONE OF YOUR PRESENTATION SLIDES TO THE ENTIRE GROUP, AND ASK EACH TABLE TO TAKE 5 MINUTES TO WRITE UP THEIR ANSWERS TO THESE QUESTIONS ABOUT THE MEGATREND THEY'VE CHOSEN ON THE FLIPCHARTS – AND HOW IT IMPACTS THEIR THINKING ON BUSINESS

7. REPEAT THIS PROCESS 8-10 TIMES

8. THEN ASK ALL TABLES TO TAKE 5 MINUTES TO SUMMARIZE THEIR FINDINGS ON A SINGLE FLIPCHART PAGE

9. ONE-BY-ONE, ASK EACH TABLE LEADER TO TAKE 2-3 MINUTES TO STAND UP AND PRESENT THEIR FINDINGS TO THE ENTIRE ROOM

10. QUICKLY SUMMARIZE THE GROUP'S FINDINGS FOR YOUR AUDIENCE, AND COLLECT FLIPCHARTS (WHICH SHOULD BE FULL OF IDEAS AND INSIGHTS) FOR LATER USE

SAMPLE QUESTIONS TO ASK YOUR AUDIENCE

Which new trends and innovations promise to most define or disrupt the shape of your chosen topic in the next 3, 5, and 10 years – and how can you quickly and effectively stay on top of them?

_____
_____
_____
_____
_____
_____
_____
_____
_____
_____
_____
_____
_____
_____
_____
_____
_____
_____
_____
_____

Where can you turn for insights into breaking developments? And what solutions can you institute that can help colleagues and/or advisers share input and collaborate at scale when they spot rising challenges or opportunities?

What areas of business are likeliest to be impacted by new innovations in your given space, to what extent, and how soon will these changes arrive?

Which business and operating models do you expect to be upended the most – and fastest – by these new developments? What types of new business and operating models will be created as a result?

What wildcards (unforeseen events) could most disrupt and alter the course of these subjects in the near- and long-term future? How can you design flexible enough business strategies to respond in turn?

The biggest paradigm shifts we currently see emerging across our industry are? How are we preparing ourselves to proactively greet them?

How are we promoting productive risk-taking across our organization, and encouraging our peers to speak up and take action more frequently in the fast of rising challenges or opportunities?

Which simple strategies can we use to quickly and successfully experiment with new ideas or initiatives – even if time and resources are sometimes hard to come by?

What are we doing to adapt to changing audience demographics – and address future generations' changing interests and needs?

What can we do to promote more diversity of thought and opinion across our organization – and incorporate more young and emerging leaders' voices into our decision-making process?

What kind of benefits is tomorrow's customer or end-user most actively seeking, and – in addition to current perks – what are some additional upsides that we could easily be offering them?

What steps are you taking to ensure that you win with every business venture (e.g. by gaining new insights and capabilities), and ensuring that – if you need to pivot – these resources can readily be applied to new ventures?

How are you finding ways to capture and deploy learning, insights, and capabilities across your full range of business investments and activities, and repurpose these tools and resources as needed to help augment or fuel other initiatives

Quick, simple ideas you could immediately start implementing to design better working strategies and adapt to future change more successfully include?

ADDITIONAL NOTES

HOW TO FUTURE-PROOF YOUR BUSINESS AND CAREER

LEAD AND SUCCEED DESPITE DISRUPTION

So much for the idea of "status quo." While modern executives are no strangers to change and disruption, it bears reminding that things only get more topsy-turvy for working professionals from here. In fact, according to recent surveys by researchers at today's top management consulting firms, no two days on the job will ever be the same again. That's because across every region of the world, and every commercial sector, market leaders explain that the only consistent theme you can count on in coming years is unpredictability.

Think you've got a handle on how fast today's business world moves? Think again. As we ourselves were shocked to find while researching recent book *Lead with Your Heart*, uncertainty is now the only certain at work; the next 10 years will bring more change than the prior 10,000; and – thanks to rapid advancements in technology and communications tools – the one thing organizational leaders can count on going forward is that they'll only be hit with more unforeseen disruptions harder, faster, and from more angles than ever before. So what's a forward-thinking executive to do if they want to help their enterprise stay ahead of the curve? Simple: Apply a simple accelerant, and learn to think faster, by changing up their leadership and management style to make leadership a concept that scales. In effect, by providing workers the insights that they need to make smarter decisions on the fly, and equipping staffers will all the tools that they need to stay better attuned to the now near-constant signals that the marketplace is sending them, it's possible to become much faster about addressing and adapting to these emerging developments in turn.

Bearing this in mind, and that business and cultural trends are now evolving at an unprecedented pace, it's no surprise that business leaders around the world note that strategic priorities for any organization hoping to get ahead in coming years must also evolve. Among the concepts they say it's now vital to champion to your staff if you want to think and move faster as an enterprise are the need to:

- Develop and maximize a globally-aware and -influenced pool of talent

- Foster a culture of employee engagement and continuous learning

- Put productivity, not process, at the heart of your operating strategy

- Dare to consistently disrupt your operations before outside forces disrupt them for you

- Make a commitment to ongoing organizational improvement

But most importantly, they also note that the best way to get ahead in uncertain times is to always be doubling down and reinvesting in your people – and that doing so can pay off in huge ways, because people are your most important asset today.

Taking this into account, today's most effective leaders realize that here and now – while things are going well, and you can most afford to take chances – is the most opportune time to start making a host of smart investments in initiatives that drive constant learning and growth for their organization. And that it's also the best time to start encouraging staffers to get behind the idea of making more insight-driven decisions, and educating themselves through a running process of trial and error that involves constantly brainstorming and testing a variety of new strategies and solutions.

Because in uncertain times, as we discovered by speaking with hundreds of market leaders, the irony is that you've got to take more risks, not fewer if you want to get ahead. However, these risks have to come in the form of small, smart, cost-effective bets designed as ongoing learning experiments that can help you quickly gain deeper insights into the shape of changing operating landscapes and make better and more informed choices as you become more knowledgeable. Likewise, to stay relevant – let alone ahead of the curve – organizations also have to start being more deliberate about putting systems and programs in place that can help frontline staffers quickly surface great ideas (whether suggested by customers, partners, or colleagues) and take on more of an ownership role in helping drive workplace decisions. Again, if you want to think and move faster, you've got to streamline your organizational structure to act as a springboard for growth – and remove the day-to-day roadblocks that often get in staffers' way.

That's because, ironically, studies of the world's most innovative firms repeatedly show that end-users – everyday customers, strategic partners, the various internal/external stakeholders that we serve, etc. – are the #1 best, most reliable proven source where organizations get successful new ideas. Given that findings also show that most of these ideas can be implemented in 30 days or less to boot, it also demonstrates that if you want to think and move faster as an enterprise, you need to stay well-attuned and responsive to these incoming signals as well. And yet, at the same time, research also tells us that less than a third of organizations have effective systems in place for capturing this feedback and using it to create winning solutions. Keeping this in mind, the real question you should be asking yourself as an executive leader going forward – and encouraging your coworkers to ask themselves – isn't "do we have what it takes to compete" at your organization. It's "are you doing everything you can to give your people all the tools and resources that they need to be listening to the signals the marketplace is constantly sending you, and promptly and intelligently responding to them in turn?"

For example, Dell EMC is a market leader in the field of IT and big data. It has over 60,000 employees worldwide. But when it has a huge, hard problem it just can't seem to solve? It aims to accelerate problem-solving by routinely putting the challenge to its employees in the form of an Innovation Contest. In effect, to quickly and cost-efficiently scale its ability to come up with winning business ventures, the company puts up a website where workers are invited to suggest ideas for innovative new solutions – and can comment on these ideas, give colleagues feedback, and vote on which of these concepts are turned into real-world prototypes and products. Ironically though, it turns out that many of the firm's most successful ventures are happening when employees worldwide are independently teaming up on their own time to bring new ideas that they found online to life – many of which weren't technically contest winners.

Likewise, you can see a host of government agencies doing a similar end-run around traditional bureaucratic and budgeting hurdles, and employing like-minded solutions for accelerating and scaling innovation, at Challenge.gov – a website where institutions like the Centers for Disease Control and Prevention and U.S. Army put up contests asking the general public and members of the private sector for help with tasks like designing better healthcare programs or building better underground bunkers. Prizes for winning solutions can often exceed $1 million – but it's often a small price to pay by these organizations, comparatively, for creating platforms that allow these agencies to radically multiply the number of winning ideas, insights, and solutions that they're able to surface.

Long story short? When it comes to getting ahead despite disruption, and finding ways to successfully navigate through change, even as an experienced team leader, it often pays to find more ways to step back and let others take the lead. The more you look to make leadership and innovation concepts that scale, and put programs and platforms in place to rapidly transform ideas into reality – say a running series of 48-hour hackathon events (in which participants must create working product prototypes in less than two days), or a six-week company-wide design contest that crowdsources concepts for new business opportunities to explore? The faster you'll be able to think and move, and more successful you'll be, no matter what the future brings.

THE NEW TOOLS LEADERS NEED TO STAY AHEAD OF THE CURVE

Succeeding in hugely disruptive environments isn't about avoiding risks. In actuality, it's actually about taking more risks—albeit calculated and controlled ones. If you study leading innovators, you'll notice something interesting: They never stop innovating, and are always exploring an array of new business strategies and ventures. That's because staying ahead of the curve and making smarter decisions in disruptive environments is largely a process of controlled speculation: Being risk-averse, not risk-free.

Essentially, market leaders actively manage innovation the same way you would manage a financial portfolio. Diversify. Monitor. Consistently readjust. This means placing multiple bets. Some of these gambles will be high risk, high reward. Some will be low risk, low return. Not all will pay off. But by pursuing all, you help grow your organization's learning and capabilities, and gain deeper insights into changing markets.

Consider that Starbucks is the world's largest chain of coffee houses. It famously describes itself as "in the people biz serving coffee, not the coffee biz serving people." The company would be crazy to upset its customers, right? But it constantly puts its Arabica beans on the line. Starbucks is routinely rolling out new business strategies and programs, such as new store concepts, products, and payment options, even before most of these concepts are finished and error-free. Why? Because it understands the power of moving faster, and says it would rather be first than flawless, make mistakes than miss an opportunity, and fall flat than fail to be swifter to establish market beachheads than rivals. And it makes a point to train its people in a simple, but hugely powerful principle that sets the business up to succeed time and again: In the face of ongoing change and disruption, the only thing to truly be afraid of is not changing as well.

Identifying Tomorrow's Leaders

Tomorrow's leaders will possess only two defining characteristics: The ability to solve problems and create results. Accordingly, it's vital to instill more bootstrapping values (for example, a culture of ownership, entrepreneurship, and accountability) in employees, and teach them how to more effectively think dynamically and solve problems in context.

Case in point: At Intuit, a personal finance software maker, senior management says its sole role now is "to remove the speed bumps in experimenters' way." To this extent, its employees are routinely encouraged to think like business owners and experiment like mad scientists, bringing new products and projects to market as fast as possible, learning from these efforts, and sharing their insights with the broader organization at large.

Workers are then encouraged to come up with still more new ideas, and use online collaboration tools to secure resources, support, and insights from peers. They then go to market with real-world prototypes as fast as possible. Intuit's employees can now do this without getting the management or legal team's approval (yet more speed bumps removed), and dozens of revenue-generating products and features have resulted.

Skills For the Future

The capabilities and tools needed to succeed in business today and tomorrow look very different from those that were needed to succeed yesterday. Below are the skills you should be teaching employees in a world where systems routinely break down, variables are constantly changing, and uncertainty is the only certain.

> - **Make smarter decisions.** Time, effort, and energy are finite resources, meaning that every decision comes with two costs: Opportunity, as well as financial. Teach employees how to factor both in when making decisions and considering which ventures to pursue. The more they consider where efforts are best focused from a long-term perspective, the more successful they'll be.

- **Manage time.** Common wisdom says that "busy is good." But truthfully, it's only good if you're spending this time steadily working toward achieving your stated goals. When deciding where to focus, teach employees to concentrate on accomplishing tasks that directly move them further toward achieving your organization's overarching objectives, and avoid becoming distracted by busywork or lower-priority demands that often cause us to lose focus on the big picture.

- **Maximize effort.** Successful leaders always find ways to win in every scenario besides pure profits. That way, they're always able to benefit from any given choice, and use what they've gained from the undertaking as a springboard to fuel continued growth and advancement. For example, by taking on a new project or client that helps you push your company's capabilities in new directions, you may gain invaluable new connections, insights, and experience into promising new avenues of growth or opportunity.

- **Focus on long-term goals.** Rather than simply concentrate on the here and now, train workers today to also be purposefully seeking out the tools, talents, and resources they'll need to succeed tomorrow. Perhaps transitioning a lower-ranking or lower-paying job role isn't such a bad idea if it gets them invaluable training and experience into emerging areas that will be in demand in the future. Likewise, maybe spending less time trying to sell more existing products and focusing on successfully launching innovative new ones is a better investment in your organization's growth capabilities as well.

- **Think fluidly.** Leaders need to learn to make firm business decisions despite uncertainty. The simplest way to do so is to exercise "strong, but weakly held opinions." Teach leaders to do their homework up front and gather as much business intelligence as possible, then act. And, after assessing the results of their choices, they should adjust their approaches to be more successful based on the insights gained from these efforts.

- **Embrace failure.** Modern successes consistently experiment with new business strategies and solutions, and aren't afraid to fail. Think of failure as the price of getting an education—a price that you can control. It's alright to fail as long as you're failing quickly and cost-effectively, and learning from mistakes and using the insights gained to improve future tries.

- **Future-proof.** To keep themselves, and your business, ahead of the curve, teach employees to prioritize ongoing education and professional development. Train them to regularly stop and ask themselves: What types of talents, training, and educational experiences will be in demand tomorrow? Then have them purposefully seek out the opportunities they'll need to get these assets right here, right now today. That way, both your organization and its workforce will be ready to greet the future long before it comes knocking.

- **Fix problems.** If your organization finds itself dealing with the same issues over and over, there's probably a larger underlying issue that keeps causing them. Encourage workers to purposefully seek these challenges out, and to stop curing symptoms and start solving problems. Instead of struggling with side effects, you will all find that it's better to fix what ails you once and be done with it.

The biggest challenges we face when it comes to getting ahead faster in business are, ironically, the same ones we often face in everyday life: Teaching ourselves and our colleagues to be more open to change, and more flexible and diligent about responding to it. So instead of fighting change, teach employees to prepare themselves to greet it more effectively, and be more amenable to rolling with the punches.

Be bold. Be creative. Be open to new perspectives. And be willing to take some smart risks. The more you can teach this formula, the more you'll give employees all the tools they need to stay in tune with changing times and trends, stay on top of their field, and stay ahead of the curve as well.

Characteristics of Future-Proof Leaders

Today's business leaders must remain focused on what's next. Here is a list of attributes those best equipped to succeed in tomorrow's working world should embody.

- **Crave curiosity.** If we want to think like futurists, it's more important to ask "why?" than "what?" so that we can dive into the root cause of an issue and understand the value shifts driving today's trends.

- **Act courageously.** Human beings are wired to reject change, and the future is synonymous with change. A good futurist must recognize that the insights we share will make others feel uncomfortable, but it is in that discomfort that growth occurs.

- **Think outrageously.** The ability to think provocatively is paramount to being able to see ahead of the curve, and react faster. To expand our thinking (and that of our leadership and stakeholders), we must stretch our minds beyond our comfort zone.

- **Connect the dots.** It is not enough to collect the dots (or trends). A forward-looking executive also must connect them to uncover patterns. To understand what's next, we must analyze the intersection of trends and make sense of the patterns they form.

- **Think in multiples.** As future-focused leaders, we must be able to think in simultaneous, multiple futures rather than the traditional, single, linear forecast. Being able to consider myriad paths beyond the official future allows us to create robust and resilient strategies that will be successful no matter which future emerges.

HOW TO FUTURE-PROOF YOUR CAREER

Constant change is the new status quo and uncertainty the only certain in business. This radical instability fundamentally undermines the foundation of traditional career advancement models, grounded in stable organizations, working environments, and job hierarchies to ascend. To ensure ongoing career growth and progression going forward, tomorrow's leaders won't just need to be more skilled and capable. They'll also need to be more forward-thinking, resilient, and able to improvise as well.

As interviews with scores of leading business researchers, academics, and senior leaders at leading startups and global innovators such as Cisco, Merck and Dell reveal though, this concept is seldom instinctive. Rather, it requires working professionals to anticipate continuous career disruption, and take calculated steps to acquire *elastic skills* – widely-applicable talents which can easily be remolded to fit any industry, organization, or job role. Capable of serving as springboards to future opportunities, these elastic skills can allow workers to become more flexible, agile, and adaptable regardless of circumstance, even as knowledge and experience steadily compound. They can also help executives rebound more effectively from unexpected setbacks. But perhaps most strikingly, the process of gaining these skills, and the invaluable insights, contacts, and experiences that often accompany them, frequently requires one to execute a series of seemingly counterintuitive career moves – often at the expense of immediate opportunities for advancement or financial gain.

To understand the new model for career success, I interviewed more than 125 serial and self-made successes, including a mix of intrapreneurs, entrepreneurs, and leadership training professionals, to see how they both fueled ongoing success in their career and prepared future leaders to greet tomorrow's challenges. As I explain in bestselling book *Make Change Work for You: 10 Ways to Future-Proof Yourself, Fearlessly Innovate, and Succeed Despite Uncertainty,* feedback indicates that the new formula for career success is simple:

- Stay ahead of shifts in your industry by constantly broadening your experience and perspective.

- Cultivate flexibility and resilience in your career.
- Be a generalist, and learn as much as you can. Learn how to learn.
- Assume that disruptions will occur, and prepare for them in advance.
- Equip yourself with the skills and resources you need to improvise.
- Be purposeful and forward-thinking about the choices you make.
- Use feedback gained from the results of your efforts to keep making more informed choices going forward.

As a simple example, one successful marketing executive we polled guards against career upheaval by taking smart risks. To accelerate growth, and become more adaptable, he routinely reviews his professional strengths and weaknesses then takes on a progression of carefully-chosen job roles that address any shortcomings, and provide compounding education and experience that serve as launchpads to future opportunities. He specifically seeks out job positions that require him to exercise new professional skills, and present him with more challenging roles and responsibilities, which allow him to grow in ability, gain new talents, and demonstrate competence in unfamiliar areas over time. This makes him more flexible and attractive to future employers, and capable of self-sustaining should he ever need to operate independently. To circumvent the onset of potential career disruptions, he routinely disrupts himself, gaining the knowledge, training and elastic skills needed to successfully adapt long before the future arrives.

Assessing survey participants' success strategies, it quickly becomes apparent that three new career moves that are equally elastic as the skills they can convey – *the sidestep, backstep, and all-important slingshot* – can further help executives sustain upward momentum, even in uncertain times. If you find your career plateauing, you can move sideways, a.k.a. *sidestep*, into a position of equal rank and pay (into an organization that offers more opportunities for advancement or career growth) or take a *backstep* by moving down the ladder and accepting a less-prestigious title or less pay (say, leaving a Fortune 500 business to work for a start-up for the chance to gain new skills and hands-on experience, or work in emerging markets). Alternately, you can take a slingshot by making both a sidestep and a backstep while staying focused on your ultimate career target: When you apply the knowledge, experience and skills gained through these moves, you'll leap far ahead.

Case in point: The executive I interviewed recently left Google to join a small, unproven start-up offering him more challenging opportunities in a more demanding role and business environment. Just over a year later, he returned to Google, vaulting himself several rungs up the ladder in terms of rank and pay via this process.

But equally important to contemporary career success as becoming more resilient is cultivating the ability to sustainably improvise. Sheryl Sandberg, author of popular book *Lean In*, suggests that the pathway to career success is a jungle gym you must traverse erratically, rather than an upward ladder to climb. However, this theory is incorrect, as it presupposes that rungs (stable, predefined opportunities, e. g. available job positions) exist to climb upon and that others have placed them there for you to utilize. Feedback from the executives I polled indicates that the process of scaling current career heights is, in fact, more like free climbing up a sheer cliff face. To ascend it, you'll constantly have to carve out your own handholds (i.e. create your own hands-on learning or job opportunities) and cling to convenient outcrops for leverage as you climb (make the most of whatever limited resources are available to drive forward momentum). Likewise, you must continually assess the odds of success for each prospective career move along the way and make the strategic choices that convey the most long-term, sustainable benefits (e.g. skills or insights you can use for a lifetime).

When career hazards bar forward progress, you cannot simply expect to find a rung conveniently placed nearby, nor is it always advisable to grab the closest one at-hand. Instead, sometimes you must circle around or even double back on your chosen route to reach your ultimate career objective. As *sidesteps, backsteps, and slingshot* maneuvers reveal, sometimes, this means having to assume a less-advanced job title in a different department (or even take a pay cut) to learn new skills or switch roles or organizations to boost opportunities for advancement.

To maneuver around unexpected stumbling blocks or dead-ends, all you can do is keep weighing the odds, considering potential payoffs, and picking the most promising new trail to follow. What's more, the only safety harness available is one that must be self-created. But if you look to the future, plan ahead, and consistently make intelligent bets that help you acquire the elastic skills, connections and resources that pave pathways to further opportunity, you can create the professional equivalent of a Bungee cord that can save you if you ever slip, and—as you begin to bounce back—also help vault you to unexpected heights.

Here's a simple illustration. One young technology executive we interviewed graduated during the Great Recession with minimal business experience and qualifications. Skeptical of a graduate degree and low-paying, dead-end jobs' ultimate value, she created her own shortcut to career success by turning her life into a self-guided MBA program. Committing five years to tackling a semester-like timeline of self-imposed challenges, including launching new conferences and entrepreneurial ventures, she purposefully declined full-time employment to pursue self-directed goals that filled in gaps in her experience and skill set. Effectively, this young professional bet that the experience, skills and professional contacts she'd gain by undertaking these exercises would outweigh a measly, entry-level paycheck.

Taking a more forward-thinking approach to career advancement, not only did she complete all her goals far ahead of schedule, and gain talents and knowledge far beyond those possessed by most peers. She proceeded to found a successful online start-up, become a noted industry thought leader, and serve as the youngest-ever member of her college's board of trustees. She says she made far safer bets than peers who passively fell back on traditional career advancement systems. Win or lose, she knew she'd increase her confidence, capabilities, and value to prospective future employers with each successive attempt.

Wherever you sit on the career spectrum, exercising resilience and improvisation can not only accelerate career growth, but help sustain it, even in the face of continued setbacks. Consider the following examples, which demonstrate the power of elastic skills and career models at work.

Three albums and a thousand shows into a thriving music career, the drummer for the gold-selling band Gravity Kills should've been living the high-life. Instead, his band was owed thousands in unpaid sales, and he was living on his wife's $24,000-a-year day job. When his publisher went bankrupt, he leveraged his love for music, ear for acoustics, and an architecture degree he had into a burgeoning career building high-end performance spaces for clients like Washington University, the St. Louis Art Museum and CBS Radio.

A successful biologist realized that he loved the social aspects of the discipline more than its scientific aspects, so he put himself through law school, only to realize six years later that it wasn't a good career fit. Carrying over elastic skills he'd acquired throughout these career shifts (including a flair for strategic planning, research, and corporate communications) into new disciplines, he now uses them to serve clients in myriad fields as the head of a thriving association management business.

Two basic principles – being proactive, purposeful, and persistent with regard to one's objectives, but highly flexible with strategic approaches – are central to modern career advancement. As researchers Siobhan O'Mahony and Beth Bechky explain through the concept of *stretchwork*, winners don't simply seek out jobs that pay the bills. Rather, they select specific occupational roles that can help them parlay competency in existing disciplines into new areas, and expand their toolbox of professional talents and capabilities, becoming more adaptable and resilient as they go over time.

Finding career success isn't about instant gratification. It's about constantly building bridges to future opportunities. As the eads of FedEx and Shell's most innovative leadership training programs suggest, the following principles can also help you sustain positive growth, even in the most highly-disruptive business environments:

> • Become essential by seeking out capabilities, insights, and training that are inherently rare and difficult to come by. The more uniquely value-adding you are, the more difficult you become to replace. As a simple illustration, you might become your company's go-to expert on resolving complex regulatory issues or IT security challenges.

- Anticipate change and change with it by consistently striving to gain on-the-job knowledge and skills that will be in-demand tomorrow today. Know where you wish to be in your career. Then consistently push yourself to learn, grow, and expand your abilities and comfort zone by pursuing opportunities that can help you get the elastic skills that can help you chart a course to this destination, however roundabout its path may be.

- Create your own luck by taking steps to put yourself in fortune's sights more frequently. Instead of exercising tired job skills time and again, look for ways to pick up new skills, or put those you already possess to new and novel purposes. Actively experiment with new business solutions, push the boundaries of your problem-solving abilities, and partner with others to spark innovation. The more you exercise your creativity, the more creative you'll be.

- Don't clock out when the workday ends. Put off-hours when others shut down to work towards your advantage by pursuing side-projects or interests that can help build experience, education, or helpful business skills.

- Differentiate by making your work portfolio your resume. That way, the next time an HR rep asks for your qualifications, instead of handing them a piece of paper that describes your experience, you can have something tangible you can point to and say "I did that."

In the same way that organizations must perpetually change and innovate to keep pace with changing circumstances and markets, so too must working professionals. To deal with impending career changes—expected or otherwise—it's essential to improvise, and think ahead. You can better equip yourself to do so by seeking out the tools, training, and expertise you need to succeed long before you need them, and consistently applying these solutions to positive effect. If you're adequately prepared to greet impending changes, the rest is all about being ready, willing and able to change as situations dictate.

HOW TO FUTURE-PROOF YOUR BUSINESS

Contrary to popular belief, future proofing your business doesn't have to be difficult, time-consuming, or expensive. Nor is coming up with future proof ideas as hard as it sounds when you make a point of regularly planning ahead in business. As briefly touched on earlier, and previous operating models remind us, discovering how to stay relevant is largely a process of consistently making simple, evolutionary changes versus chasing revolutionary leaps forward in business. Following, you'll find seven simple strategies that can help you fast-track growth and innovation, and give your organization all the capabilities it needs to stay ahead of the curve.

1. Listen to Your Customers – As discussed previously, customers are the most reliable source where organizations looking to future-proof themselves can routinely turn to discover winning new ideas. Ironically though, less than a third of businesses today have formal solutions in place for actively tracking the feedback that shoppers are sending, let alone translating it into actionable strategy. Tools such as polls, surveys, questionnaires, market research, and social media monitoring software (for tracking popular topics and conversational trends) can all help you surface invaluable insights here. But if you truly want to successfully mine today's most consistent source of winning business ideas for great concepts, including clever and cost-effective ways to stay relevant? It also pays to embrace the concept of "open innovation," or regularly putting out calls for help to partners, suppliers, and even the general public. In effect, the more you invite input from outside sources of every kind, the more you can radically multiply the amount of insights and resources available to you – and the speed at which you can solve any challenge.

2. Encourage Employees to Speak Up – As those closest to customers on a running basis, external-facing workers of every kind (e.g. sales reps, customer service specialists, community managers, field service technicians, etc.) are often an organization's most well-informed audience. Therefore, if you want to future-proof your business, it's also vital to find ways to tap into their insights at every turn. Noting this, it's no surprise that today's most successful businesses don't just make a point to put platforms and programs in place that facilitate teamwork and collaboration, and give workers a greater voice in making decisions, across the board. They also actively work to promote cultures of trust and respect in which everyone is encouraged to speak up and share their input, and reward contributors for bringing both potential opportunities and challenges to the organization's attention. Likewise, to build and maintain competitive advantage, these firms consistently provide their people with the systems and support that they need to quickly translate ideas into action – and make leadership a concept that scales at every level.

3. Freely Collaborate with Peers. Want to move faster? Make a point to flatten lines of communication in your enterprise, and allow information, insights and support to flow freely throughout your organization. The more readily you can align tools, talent and resources toward achieving common goals, the more readily you can foster innovation. Case in point: Germany's Association for Chemistry and Economics (VCW) has over 30,000 members spread across hundreds of industries. Knowing that teamwork would be crucial to successfully managing change, and accelerating the speed at which it could adapt, VCW wanted to create a solution that would allow these members to more easily connect and collaborate to help drive ongoing innovation on a huge scale. So the organization coined the concept of "Social Chemistry" and built a website that allowed members to crowdsource ideas, team up with talent from outside the field, and pool resources across public and private organizations. Within just 5 weeks, the VCW had produced hundreds of ideas, sparked dozens of new initiatives for the industry, and helped identify several trends which weren't even on the association's radar. Ask yourself: What's stopping you from doing similar?

4. Spread Your Risk – Leading organizations don't try to be risk-free, but rather risk-averse, and actively pursue a more calculated range of business bets. As with financial portfolios, these enterprises constantly manage and adjust a portfolio of strategic ventures. Not all wagers will pan out. But all are designed to collectively help the organization grow its capabilities, spread risk, and learn through real-time monitoring and course correction. For example: Market leaders like Sony and Microsoft specifically commit teams to pushing the boundaries of technology in new directions, knowing that these new developments may be put to a variety of useful business purposes — not all of them commercial. Similarly, in good times, your organization can also plan for bad times by routinely rolling out new ventures and solutions that offer the potential for evolution, growth, and expansion as well. Market leaders are constantly using innovation laboratories and incubators to play a portfolio of investments and wagers. You can do the same.

5. Iterate, Don't Reinvent – Innovation isn't always about coming up with game-changing concepts. In fact, simple shifts in communications or operations strategy can be every bit as successful at helping you create huge windfalls for your business. Ask yourself: How could you reuse existing resources, capabilities, or solutions in new and exciting ways – or repackage them to appeal to new audiences? What could your organization do in a single step that's currently taking it several steps to perform – or where could technology help you automate or skip these steps entirely? In essence, innovation (like future-proofing) is largely a matter of perspective, and process of constant reimagining and reinvention. The more frequently you make a point to challenge yourself and your people to think differently, the more innovative (and, ultimately, future proof) you'll be.

6. See Tomorrow Today – Rather than simply keep pace with rivals, top innovators always consider where the future is heading and strive to put the solutions tomorrow's audiences will demand in place today. For instance: Google, HP and 3M are famous for encouraging employees to invest large portions of paid time exploring fresh ideas and experimenting with new innovations. As opposed to standard maintenance and upkeep tasks — i.e. research, marketing, member services, etc. — how much of your organization and its staff's time are you investing in long-term growth activities designed to expand its reach and capabilities? To help bridge the gap from here to there strategically, provide workers with the freedom to take lots of small, cost-productive risks that have the potential to pay off for the business from a long-term perspective, learning as they go. Similarly, on an organizational level, make it a priority to play a portfolio of new strategic ventures at all times, optimizing and course-correcting as you gather and learn from market feedback along the way. Remember, not every new venture will pan out. But just by pursuing this process of constant evolution, you'll help actively grow your business' capabilities and insights, and improve its ability to shift with changing markets over time.

7. Challenge Every Assumption – Ironically, if you're still doing things the way they've "always been done" on the job, it pays to remind yourself: As fast as today's business world changes and evolves, odds are that they are no longer the best way to still be doing them. Keeping in mind that competitors are always looking for ways to do things better, faster, and cheaper, it's crucial to routinely challenge your people to look for ways to proactively disrupt yourself before you get disrupted by other parties. That's why it's important to always be experimenting with new innovations and solutions, as above, especially while things are going well, and you can most afford to take risks. The more you make a point to actively push yourself to try new approaches or strategies, and challenge longstanding assumptions, the more future-proof your business (and its ideas) will ultimately be.

Ultimately, building a future-proof business, and determining how to stay relevant, isn't about having all the answers up-front. Rather, it's about being more open-minded and resilient, and taking a more forward-thinking approach to your operating strategy – as well as remaining self-aware enough to know when to rip up and/or rewrite the plan as you go.

7 HABITS OF HUGELY SUCCESSFUL ORGANIZATIONS

According to top researchers, continuous change is the new norm in business. To stay relevant in a fast-changing world, leaders must continually change and innovate as well. As research with scores of leading innovators for our bestselling book *Make Change Work for You* reveals though, this process doesn't need to be difficult.

Studies of the world's most-innovative firms show that their key source of competitive advantage is merely providing workers with better platforms for speaking up, sharing insights, and taking action. These businesses' leading source of new ideas is simply listening to customers as well—another area where frontline employees are best poised to spot rising opportunities.

Clearly, corporate culture plays a pivotal role in driving innovation. Following are seven new habits that can help you adapt yours to be more competitive – and stay ahead of highly-disruptive business environments:

- **Create a culture of trust and encourage employees to speak up.** Leading organizations empower workers and reward them for bringing potential opportunities and challenges to their attention. Frontline employees are often an enterprise's most informed audience—to create and sustain competitive advantage, provide them the tools they need to translate ideas into action.

- **Constantly rethink business practices.** Is the way it's always been done" still the best way to do it? Like competitors, market leaders are always asking themselves this question.

- **Freely collaborate across the organization.** Flatten lines of communication, and allow information, insights and support to flow throughout your enterprise. The more readily you can align tools, talent and resources towards common goals, the more readily you can foster innovation.

- **See the future today.** Rather than simply keep pace with rivals, top innovators always consider where the future is heading and strive to put the solutions tomorrow's audiences will demand in place today.

- **Be open to change.** Leaders expect employees to stay abreast of changing business environments—and intelligently and flexibly respond to them. To this extent, workers are given the freedom to take small, smart risks that have the potential to help the organization better serve its customers… so long as these risks are intelligent, productive, and cost-affordable.

- **Spread your risk.** Leading organizations don't try to be risk free, but rather actively pursue a more calculated range of business bets. As with financial portfolios, these enterprises constantly manage and adjust a portfolio of strategic ventures. Not all wagers will pan out. But all are designed to collectively help the organization grow its capabilities, spread risk, and learn through real-time monitoring and course-correction.

- **Never stop learning.** Rather than just rely solely on contingency plans, market leaders consistently experiment with new innovations and solutions—especially when things are going well, and they can most afford to gamble. By consistently pioneering new ideas and approaches, and extending their experience, capabilities and comfort zones, they create added flexibility and room to maneuver in the face of changes or unforeseen events.

In short, leading organizations turn employees into emergency responders. They transform infrastructures from barriers into enablers. They see business strategy as being flexible, not fixed. And they continually provide workers with the tools and runway they need to reimagine, reinvent, and innovate their way to success as scenarios change. You too can consistently innovate, succeed, and go from strength to strength, by doing the same.

How To Successfully Innovate

• Constantly look for ways to expand you and your organization's capabilities and comfort zones. The more learning and experience you can bring to bear, the more adaptable you'll be.

• Reconsider the solutions you offer. Could you give yourself more room to maneuver by providing your expertise to new audiences, or repackaging or remixing them to expand avenues of opportunity?

• Rather than compete on cost or speed alone, compete to differentiate yourself from rivals. The more unique your solutions, the harder you'll be to replace, and more of a premium you'll command.

• Treat relevancy and value as moving targets: Stay attuned to changing market needs, and constantly tinker with both business strategies and ways to get out in front of shifting customer demands.

• When weighing choices, don't forget to factor in opportunity costs. Sometimes, decisions that come at greater short-term expense may provide greater long-term gains.

WHAT'S HOLDING YOU BACK FROM SUCCESS?

Research shows the #1 barrier to ongoing business success isn't time, money, or resources: It's resistance to change, and lack of risk tolerance. As fast-moving and unpredictable as today's world is though, we're all forced to adapt on a daily basis. Haven't taken a good look at your shifting schedule or priorities lately? Surprise – chances are, you're successfully changing and innovating every day already. If *everyone* is capable of innovating, the only thing stopping you from getting ahead consistently is your own sense of perspective. As we discovered, fear comes in seven flavors. Learn to conquer them, and you'll soon find out – the possibilities are endless.

#1: FEAR OF FAILURE
The possibility of being unable to successfully complete a goal or task set by yourself or others.

Solution: Experiment frequently. Fail fast and often, but fail smartly—use failure as a way to cost-affordably experiment with strategies and solutions to course-correct as you go, until you find success. Just don't make the same mistakes twice.

#2: FEAR OF EMBARASSMENT
The shame and self-consciousness felt when one feels humiliated, unable to live up to expectations, or socially conform.

Solution: Start trying and doing new things, expanding you and your organization's comfort zone, making small steps until you feel comfortable pursuing larger ones.

#3 – FEAR OF LOSING CONTROL
Fear of losing control. Believing that situations and events have spiraled beyond our ability to command or adapt to them.

Solution: Accept that certain variables are beyond your control. Instead, focus on controlling those you have the power to manage.

#4 – FEAR OF REJECTION

When you, your organization, or your products or services are refused, turned away, or avoided by others.

Solution: Maintain confidence and keep forging ahead. You're going to hear "no" more often than "yes" in life. The more you hear it, the closer you're statistically getting to yes, and things have in business, no often simply means "no for now"—don't hesitate to try later, as circumstances change.

#5 – FEAR OF CONFRONTATION

Experiencing a negative event or having a hostile personal or professional interaction with others.

Solution: Stop avoiding confrontation and face problems—take a step back, think about the best way to tackle them, then begin addressing them one step at a time, updating your strategy based on the results your actions produce.

#6 – FEAR OF ISOLATION

The feeling of being alone or left to operate on your own without others' support.

Solution: Build your own strategies while also building trust and strong relationships with colleagues. Be part of a team, but be yourself as well.

#7 – FEAR OF CHANGE AND UNCERTAINTY

The process of acting or reacting differently—and the discomfort that accompanies these shifts and/or surrounding uncertainties or risks.

Solution: Don't try to predict the future. Instead, study events as they take shape, and adapt. Design a portfolio of small, smart professional bets to take – bets in the form of changing decisions and actions. Constantly revise these bets as you gain new information, and adapt your strategies accordingly.

THE NEW RULES OF CAREER SUCCESS

Ever feel like the corporate ladder is broken? That's because you're making the mistake of trying to climb it. As we discovered through our research, an increasingly uncertain business world requires all-new methods of thinking and strategies to navigate. Following are eight new rules needed for professional success in increasingly unpredictable career environments – and how to use them to vault yourself straight into the executive suite.

Become Essential – You've got to be crucial to your organization – not someone that's easily replaced. For example: You might be the company's go-to IT expert, a crucial member of its engineering team, or a highly sought-after internal thought leader. If others can do what you do, you're already on the road to irrelevance. Instead, be a lynchpin, or crucial piece in any system – one that's fundamentally difficult and expensive to replace.

Rethink Your Value – Never stop learning, improving, and investing in yourself – then consistently apply these talents in ways that go far beyond your job description. For example: If you're a programmer, take design and marketing classes so you can create more user-friendly and engaging products. If you're a marketer, spend more time with your programmers so you can find new ways to leverage your creative ideas through technology. The more versatile you make yourself, the more adaptable, resourceful and uniquely value-adding you can be.

Change and Evolve – Get the capabilities, skills and insights today that will be in-demand tomorrow. Take steps to acquire the talents, contacts and resources you'll need to succeed in the future, so you can be in a more advantageous position to greet it when it arrives. Know where you want to go in your career, have a plan for getting there, and voluntarily push yourself to learn, grow and take on more leadership and responsibility – even if this means taking small steps in different directions until bigger ones become more comfortable.

Create Your Own Opportunities – Go, see, try and do. Put yourself into situations that place you outside your comfort zone, like taking on unfamiliar tasks that require you to do new things with new people. Be open-minded, and soak up as much knowledge and learning as you can – then apply it vigorously. The more you do so, the more you'll consistently put yourself in opportunity's path and the greater your chances of finding it will be.

Never Stop Learning – Constantly look for ways to expand your education and insights – the most resilient leaders are eternal students, and possess talent and training that's applicable to a wide range of professional contexts. Think of it this way: The more resources you've got in your professional toolkit, and ways you can use them, the more future-proof you'll be.

Embrace Difficult Challenges – Seek out hard tasks that others avoid: It means you've got less competition, and the benefits of accomplishing these tasks will be more singular and value. Look to apply a variety of skills and insights while doing so too: The more you exercise different talents while others exercise the same ones over and over, the more versatile you'll be. Applying focused effort towards accomplishing larger goals can help you achieve more. And the more you push your comfort zone, the more you'll increase your courage and capabilities.

Go Above and Beyond – What personal activities are you pursuing that can teach you marketable skills, or push you closer towards achieving your career goals? Going forward, your work, your reputation, and your contributions will be your résumé—use off-hours opportunities as a chance to grow and enhance them, and set yourselves apart while others shy away from opportunity.

Take Smart Risks – The more you do the same things over time, the less value they hold in a rapidly-changing world. Faced with change, you've got to take risks that can help propel you further towards achieving your goals. But being risky doesn't necessarily mean being reckless: Rather, smarter about where you place your bets. Pick a portfolio of promising growth activities – start a part-time business, launch a new product, volunteer to lead an innovative new venture, etc. – then pursue them, readjusting your strategies as you go based on the results achieved. Keep taking promising risks that put you in chance's sights, and put you in a position to succeed.

WHY INNOVATION IS SIMPLER THAN YOU THINK

Who says innovation has to be difficult? While game-changing breakthrough technologies and new scientific discoveries tend to hog media headlines, it bears remembering: Evolutionary changes (slight shifts in business strategy or thinking) can often be every bit as powerful as revolutionary advancements. All too often, at the pace today's market moves, and scale on which market leaders operate, we often forget – all it frequently takes to get ahead is just a minor shift in tactics or perspective.

For example:

When L&T General Insurance – a full-service health, property, and casualty insurance provider – wanted to find a way to serve the hugely-diverse and hugely-scattered Indian market? Instead of applying a Western business model and attempting to install branches in every remote town and village and hoping customers would come to it, the company took a contrarian approach. Rather than leverage traditional market strategies, it flipped them on their heads, equipping insurance agents with smartphones and tablets on which a suite of online, cloud-based apps capable of issuing policies and processing claims on the spot was preinstalled, so that agents could go to customers instead.

When medical device leader Medtronic wanted to expand its already successful business throughout Western Europe and beyond? It didn't double-down on cutting-edge devices. It reinvented its business model instead, expanding its offerings to include services, and establishing new business units that partnered to put owned-and-operated labs inside hospitals.

Not only has Medtronic increased its business and provided partners with significant improvements in customer service and cost-savings by doing so. Having earned their trust, it's also built a sizable business around ancillary services such as supply chain management and performance benchmarking.

When French telecom giant Orange wanted to double the size of its innovation initiatives, but didn't want to invest millions in R&D or hordes of high-priced working professionals? It decided to outsource the entire process, and offered APIs – plug-and-play back-end software solutions – both to internal employees and external developers so that they could create new uses for Orange's technologies. Using just one of these solutions, the company has been able to seamlessly integrate social and second-screen experiences from hundreds of film and TV companies into many of its services in under a year.

When Newell Rubbermaid's Contigo brand wanted to find a way to differentiate its products in the hugely-crowded and -contested market for portable containers and cups? It didn't invest a fortune into dozens of abortive product roll-outs, attempting to guess what working professionals on the go would want. It simply studied today's busiest travel sites, where commuters tended to congregate and – after discovering that passengers were constantly wiping off their mugs' mouth guards on napkins, sleeves, and handkerchiefs – it introduced a new line of travel mugs with special covers designed to keep out dirt.

And when MasterCard needed a new idea for a mobile payment app? It simply put the call out to employees at Innovation Express, a global series of hackathon events where businesspeople, designers, and software developers team up to create new business plans and products in record time. Two days later, Qkr – which can let you order food from your seat at a stadium, or preorder school lunches for children right from your pocket without ever setting foot in a cafeteria – was born.

While it's not always obvious to the casual observer, innovation is far easier than you think. All it takes to successfully outmaneuver the competition, or overcome a problem, is simply a greater sense of perspective, and greater willingness to be more creative with how you apply the tools at-hand.

HOW TO PLAN FOR BAD TIMES IN GOOD

The modern marketplace has entered a period of unprecedented volatility, with over 22 million workers recently unemployed, and nearly nine in ten businesses currently struggling, according to recent surveys. As the aftermath of the coronavirus and resulting economic ripples remind, the only thing we can predict as working professionals is growing unpredictability going forward. Noting this, as any futurist can tell you, right here, right now (while things are relatively good, and there's still time to get ahead of any potential commercial downswings) is the absolute best time to start hedging your bets against disruption.

Below, you'll find several steps that you'll want to immediately take as an executive leader to guard against potential drop-offs in business, and strategies that you can start applying to offset potential declines in revenue. By making a point to engage in all, and actively plan for bad times in good, you'll not only help bolster your business' resources and resilience, and give yourself a stronger position to fall back on if hard times arrive. You'll also gain the flexibility and agility that you need as an organization in order to quickly pivot operating strategies or springboard to new opportunities if the marketplace takes a sudden, unexpected turn.

Secure More Favorable Payment and Financing Terms – Cash flow (specifically, lack thereof) is one of the largest threats to your business. You can improve yours by taking this time to negotiate better payment and financing terms (e.g. allowing you to pay bills in 90 days vs. 30), or temporary discounts and deals, with suppliers and vendors. Likewise, you can accelerate the amount of funds coming in the door by offering clients discounts on preorders for products and services, or pricing specials (i.e. a 5%-off coupon) if their outstanding invoices are paid more rapidly, such as within 10 days from issuance. Time before potential dips in the market hit can also be used to negotiate with lenders and landlords regarding temporary suspensions in interest or rent payments, including implanting a working plan for how you'll eventually repay these sums.

Build Out Your Credit Options – Having lines of credit you can call on if money gets tight can help you out in a pinch. Now's a good time to speak with lenders (including your credit card company) and up the maximum amount you can borrow, before a potential downswing in business strikes. While it's not always necessary to tap into these resources, having backup reserves may come in handy if times get lean, especially if other businesses feeling the pinch themselves unexpectedly extend financing terms or withhold payment. Similarly, it's the right time to begin saving more of any money that comes in the door, and setting aside a 30-50% cushion for future expenses. Remember: Regardless of what the terms on any given invoice say, during times of market decline, clients may delay payment, even as your own bills begin to come due, and customer activity can drop off with scant notice.

Reduce Unnecessary Overhead and Expenses – If a purchase doesn't serve a vital purpose, get it off your balance sheet. If a more affordable option exists for getting a task completed with similar time and quality standards, make the switch. Similarly, before a market downswing hits is an opportune time to start pivoting away from long-term contracts to pay-as-you-go services and on-demand business solutions. While doing so may cost you more on an individual per-task basis, these expenditures are far less risky than keeping a fixed, long-term expense on your books. In addition, look for areas of your current operations – e.g. online payment processing or website hosting – where affordable, high-quality alternatives exist that you could quickly implement instead. For example: From search engine marketing to foreign language translations, many online marketplaces provide access to prebuilt solutions or value-priced providers that can help with recurring business needs at a fraction of your current costs.

Employ Flexible Staffing Solutions – It's not uncommon to see companies rush to downsize in difficult times. But before you consider laying off staff, remember that a number of alternate solutions can potentially help you avoid reducing headcount. For example, you might: Reduce workers' hours; implement furloughs; ask employees if you can stretch out salary payments; put bonuses and incentives on-hold temporarily; or institute a small company-wide pay cut across the board. Alternately, you might also assign employees more responsibilities to help boost productivity and increase their impact on the bottom line. In addition, many businesses are increasingly outsourcing certain needs to freelance contractors, taking on interns, and crowdsourcing contributions as a means to cut costs as well. Furthermore, you might also choose to temporarily forego a portion of your own salary, or setup a fund to help teammates in need, as many executives keen to lead by example have done.

Focus on Scenario Planning – Scenario planning is the exercise of asking yourself a simple question: What if? For example: What if customers make the switch from physical to online retail en masse, or what if car sales or live event ticket spending suddenly plunges in the wake of rising unemployment rates? Think ahead and plot out trends and events that are likely to occur over the next 6-12 months, as well as their potential impact on your business. Then brainstorm additional wildcards – e.g. a sudden downturn in the economy or second wave of viral outbreak – that could impact how the market for the products, services, or solutions that you offer develops. Once done, consider how the future is likely to look for your industry, and the role you can play within it. Then work backwards to determine which business strategies are likeliest to help you safely bridge the gap from your current operating reality to this future state.

Determine Where to Refocus and Reinvest – Market downturns and recessions are scary times, leading many businesses to quickly abandon plans and pull back spending habits. But if you've been planning for these downturns in advance, and socking away a healthy nest egg for a rainy day, like experts advise? In actuality, it's a fine time to spend on growing your resources and capabilities, since your money goes further, and ramp up your market presence to heighten awareness while competitors go silent. In other words, the best defense, as they say, is a good offense. Ask yourself: Where do growth opportunities currently exist? Where could you be making a promotional splash? Are there new markets you be entering, or ways to better position preexisting products or services to meet customers' changing needs? During times of declining financial performance, the more competitors retreat, the more they create opportunities for you to build competitive advantage and advance. What's more, now's also a fine time to focus on internal improvements such as process optimization and employee training as well.

As you can see, market downturns can be intimidating for many organizations. But even when they do arise, no one says that these market pullbacks have to be a showstopper for your business. With a little advance planning, and a little ingenuity, you can ultimately come out ahead of adversity just by teaching yourself to lean in and look for ways to make the most of an otherwise challenging situation.

SEEING TOMORROW TODAY

As you can see, training yourself to get better about learning to spot the future taking shape is far simpler and far less time-consuming that it seems at first blush. More than anything else, it's simply a question of putting yourself in a forward-thinking mindset, and actively getting in the habit of asking yourself more pointed questions. The more you actively work to exercise the skills and strategies outlined here, and build a robust network of collaborators, the more successful you'll ultimately be.

I'd love to hear more about how you are implementing these strategies in your workplace and career. Please feel free to reach out at www.AKeynoteSpeaker.com with your thoughts anytime, or follow us on Facebook, LinkedIn, or Twitter (@akeynotespeaker) to pick up even more insights on how to steer your business towards a brighter future. I look forward to learning more about the methodologies and solutions you're using to stay ahead of the curve – and how you're leveraging them to create positive results in life and business at every turn.

-Scott Steinberg

ACKNOWLEDGEMENTS

Bob, Tim, Neil, Pete, Mike, Stephane, Sue, Sandeep, Richard, Karen, Jamie, Lisa, Tamara, Eric, and Jean – thanks for always encouraging us to look towards the future, and think two steps ahead.

ABOUT THE AUTHOR

Hailed as The Master of Innovation by Fortune magazine, and the World's Leading Business Strategist, award-winning professional speaker Scott Steinberg is among today's best-known trends experts and futurists. A strategic adviser to four-star generals, government leaders, and a who's-who of Fortune 500s, he's helped craft dozens of business strategies and product designs for the world's top brands, and is the bestselling author of 14 books including Make Change Work for You: 10 Ways to Future-Proof Yourself, Fearlessly Innovate, and Succeed Despite Uncertainty, The Business Etiquette Bible, and Millennial Marketing: Bridging the Generation Gap. The President and CEO of BIZDEV: The Intl. Association for Business Development and Strategic Planning™ and founder of critically-acclaimed travel + lifestyle trends magazine SELECT: Your City's Secrets Unlocked™, his website is www.AKeynoteSpeaker.com. Named one of America's top futurists by the BBC and a "top trendsetter to follow" by the Fortune 500, this leading business insider and analyst has covered consumer, business, and lifestyle trends for 600+ outlets from CNN to Rolling Stone.

HOW FUTURE-PROOF STRATEGIES CAN HELP

- BUSINESS STRATEGY CONSULTING
- KEYNOTE SPEECHES + BREAKOUTS
- VIRTUAL PRESENTATIONS + WEBINARS
- ONLINE TRAINING + CLASSES
- MARKET RESEARCH + TREND REPORTS
- FUTURIST THINK TANKS + PANELS
- CONTENT MARKETING + EDITORIAL SERVICES

www.AKeynoteSpeaker.com

ADDITIONAL NOTES

ADDITIONAL NOTES

ADDITIONAL NOTES

ADDITIONAL NOTES

www.ingramcontent.com/pod-product-compliance
Lightning Source LLC
Chambersburg PA
CBHW021452210526
45463CB00002B/748